BACKPACKER

Backpacking

Basics

Planning, Preparing, and Packing

Clyde Soles

FALCONGUIDES

GUILFORD, CONNECTICUT
HELENA, MONTANA

AN IMPRINT OF GLOBE PEQUOT PRESS

To buy books in quantity for corporate use
or incentives, call **(800) 962-0973**
or e-mail **premiums@GlobePequot.com**.

FALCONGUIDES®

Photos by Clyde Soles unless otherwise noted.
Text design and layout: Sheryl P. Kober
Project editor: David Legere

Library of Congress Cataloging-in-Publication Data

Soles, Clyde, 1959-
  Backpacker magazine's backpacking basics : planning, preparing, and packing/
Clyde Soles.
    p. cm. — (Falconguides)
  Includes index.
  ISBN 978-0-7627-5549-3
  1. Backpacking—Handbooks, manuals, etc. 2. Camping—Handbooks, manuals,
etc. I. Backpacker. II. Title.
  GV199.6.S65 2011
  796.51—dc22

                              2010034386

Printed in China

10 9 8 7 6 5 4 3 2 1

Contents

Backpacking is a great activity that can take you to some of the world's most beautiful places. Stephen Gorman

Chapter One
Introduction to Backpacking

Backpacking has gone from an age when discomfort was the expectation to one in which trailside luxuries enhance the experience.

When I started backpacking in the early 1970s, it was perfectly normal to carry a 60-plus-pound external-frame pack the size of a small refrigerator for a few nights out. If it rained, we pulled on a poncho or, if you were serious, a waterproof cagoule that hung below the knees. In cool weather, we wore scratchy wool everything and protected ourselves from wind and snow with a heavy cotton-nylon-blend jacket. Our feet were shod with heavy leather boots that took months to break in, though it was mostly our feet that ultimately succumbed. It took dozens of stakes to pitch our A-frame tents, and they still elicited little sleep in a storm. Since there weren't many options on the market, much of our gear was made at home on mom's sewing machine.

Nowadays, with a little prudent shopping, it is quite reasonable to carry a svelte 30-pound pack for a multiday hike. The clothing, for good weather and bad, is actually comfortable and performs well when used properly. Even "heavy" boots are half the weight and break in faster, while many people don't even need that much protection. Tents set up easily and provide superior protection, even in howling gales.

Backpacking today is easier and more comfortable than ever. Of course, the trails are just as steep and the miles just as long, but the new gear truly makes them melt under your feet. If you are of the persuasion that life is too short not to be enjoyed, it is now possible to pack in a gourmet meal, and even a fine wine, to remote locations with incredible views. Or you can trim your pack down to the bare necessities for fast and light trips into distant ranges that would require many extra days with old-school technology.

While proper gear selection and usage is vital to a happy backpacking experience, there are also many tricks of the trail that will make your hikes safer and more comfortable. These are most important when venturing outside of your home region, where you may be less familiar with environmental hazards.

In this book, we will give you an overview of your equipment options in different categories, looking first at basic backpacking gear such as packs, tents, sleeping bags, and accessories. Then we will discuss clothing options for a variety of environmental conditions. In the chapters on food and water, meal basics, stoves, cook gear, and the importance of hydration and various options for water treatment are covered.

The chapter on trip planning can help you head off problems before they arise and ensure a pleasant getaway. And since most of your time is typically spent in camp, we will discuss how to enhance that part of your experience while minimizing your impact on the land. Finally, we will discuss topics unique to higher mountain ranges and arid deserts, both of which have their own hazards and unique rewards.

There is a lot of information presented in these pages, but I cannot hope to cover everything and some discussions are necessarily brief. Other titles in this Backpacker series—such as *Campside Cooking, Trailside Navigation, Predicting Weather,* and *Outdoor Knots*—offer deeper background. Since equipment is constantly evolving, consulting *Backpacker* magazine is prudent before making buying decisions to get the latest advice.

People go backpacking for many reasons. Some like to get away from the city, others wish to explore, and many enjoy it for mental and physical fitness. My own motivation has often been photography. But the common theme for everyone is having fun. The more pleasurable the experience, the more you will do it. Hopefully you will also share the rewards of wilderness with future generations and embrace the protection of the environment we share.

Chapter Two

Equipment

Perhaps you've heard the expression "a pound off your feet is equal to five pounds off your back." The corollary is "lighter is better but silly light is dumber." Gear enters the domain of "silly light" when it falls apart, fails to keep you warm and dry, or when a couple of ounces can make a dramatic increase in comfort.

When it comes to pack weight, the Big Three are your shelter, your sleeping system, and your pack. If you want to significantly reduce the load that you carry, these are where the easiest savings can be achieved.

After these major items, it helps to have a decent scale since the savings will be in ounces instead of pounds. But the ounces do add up and you won't have to go to extremes such as cutting a toothbrush handle in half or trimming the edges off topo maps. Long experience has taught me to never trust manufacturer's weights when it comes to what you actually carry. If you keep track of your base pack weight (everything minus the clothes on your back and food, water, and fuel) on different trips, you will learn where cuts can safely be made.

Consider backpacking equipment an investment in yourself. In the long run, it is usually less expensive to purchase higher quality gear that will handle your needs for years to come. Buying cheaper products that perform poorly and soon require upgrades can be a costly mistake.

TENTS

The first decision in picking an appropriate tent is deciding how many people you need to accommodate. Typically, a two-person tent offers the greatest versatility since it is light enough for solo trips and roomy enough for car camping too. Larger three- to four-person tents can offer a good weight-to-volume ratio for families; however, they also require a lot of flat, open space, which can sometimes be difficult to find.

If you will be backpacking in regions with considerable rain, then be sure to look for a roomy vestibule that can shelter your gear and allow cooking. A big vestibule is also important if you hike with dogs—a wet, muddy pooch does not make a pleasant tent mate.

In general, backpacking tents fall into one of three categories: double-wall domes, double-wall tunnels, and ultralight single walls. Double-wall tents have an outer fly of waterproof fabric that covers an inner tent made of bug-proof mesh and ripstop fabrics. These offer the greatest versatility and comfort since you can leave the fly off on starry nights, and the design reduces condensation to a bare minimum. Single-wall tents can be significantly lighter, but they rely on airflow to keep you dry.

A convertible double-wall dome tent offers greater flexibility but is heavier than a single-wall dome.

Dome tents feature two, three, or four intersecting poles (the more poles, the stronger the tent but also the heavier) and resemble an igloo. It is actually a misnomer to call dome tents "freestanding" because I have never seen one that doesn't require at least three or four stakes for proper performance. Dome tents do provide the greatest livability, particularly when cooped up inside during a storm, and you can easily pick them up to relocate. Due to their shape, domes also perform the best when winds come from multiple directions. For these reasons, a double-wall dome tent is likely your best buy when starting out.

Tunnel tents have two or three nonintersecting hoops, like a Conestoga wagon, and rely entirely

This tunnel tent with a large vestibule provides a lot of living space for minimal weight.

on front and rear stakes for support. These provide maximal space with minimal weight because they contour to the body (low and narrow at the feet, wide and tall at the hips, lower and narrower at the head). When well staked, tunnel tents can be quite storm worthy; however, side winds and heavy snow can be problematic.

Single-wall tents come in all sorts of shapes, but the most common for backpacking are A-frame styles that rely on trekking poles for support. While remarkably lightweight, these tents often require many stakes and careful pitching. Without adequate ventilation, there will be considerable condensation by morning that can soak sleeping bags. Because of these issues, and the fragile fabrics used, a single-wall tent is probably not a good choice for your first tent.

Whether double or single wall, one of the major innovations in tent construction in recent years is the advent of silicone-treated nylon fabrics (called silnylon). Compared to traditional urethane-coated fabrics, silnylons can be far lighter yet stronger, reducing tent weights considerably. The main trade-off is higher cost. Since silnylon is very slippery, some people apply seam sealer to the floor for traction to keep sleeping pads in place.

No matter the style, there is no such thing as a "four-season" tent unless you always camp in the tropics. A tent that is warm enough and sturdy enough for winter camping is far too hot and heavy for backpacking in the summer. Even the "convertible" tents that strip down for warm weather tend to be several pounds heavier than a true summer tent yet only marginally adequate for winter; they are best in spring and fall.

When comparing weights of tents in catalogs, ignore the "minimal weight" because it is so stripped down that the tent is useless (read the fine print). The most accurate number is actually the "packaged weight" since that is closer to what you will end up carrying on the trail. As a rule of thumb, a two-person backpacking tent should have a packaged weight of no more than 6 pounds, and less than 5 pounds is preferable.

Many tents now have a fast-packing option if you purchase the matching groundcloth (sometimes called a footprint). This allows the fly to be set up while leaving the tent body at home, saving several pounds. It sounds nice, but I find that either I want the bug and storm protection or I'd rather have a view of the stars.

Rather than purchase a custom footprint to protect your tent floor from abrasion, you can save money and around a half pound by using a thin sheet of plastic or Tyvek. Simply buy a rectangle at a hardware store that is large enough to fit under your tent and vestibule, and then trim it slightly smaller so that rain will not pool under your tent.

The accessories that come with most tents are frequently inadequate for the backcountry. For example, the stuff sack will be far too small once the tent is wet from rain or condensation. The skewers provided are often a cheap grade of aluminum that bends at the mere sight of a rock. Guy lines made of black cord are ideal for tripping you at night; white is better but reflective cord rules.

Two alternatives to a traditional tent are tarps and camping hammocks. When bugs are not an issue, a silnylon tarp can offer very lightweight rain shelter that is easy to pitch among trees; just string a taut ridge line and stake out the corners. However,

A camping hammock gives one person protection from bugs and rain and can be set up in locations too rugged for tents.

the weight savings are negated if you must carry mosquito netting, and they are impractical above tree line. Other tarps might be set up using trekking poles; the advantage here is that any time you can use one item for two purposes, you are saving weight.

Hammocks designed for camping simply require two stout trees, so there is virtually no impact on the terrain, and even rocky slopes are not a problem. These are strictly one-person affairs, and emptying your bladder during the night is problematic. Not for everyone, hammocks can be a good choice for "stealth camping" since you don't need a normal tent site.

This tarp tent uses trekking poles for support to reduce weight to a minimum. When conditions warrant, an optional floor and bug-proof inner tent can be carried.

SLEEPING BAGS AND PADS

The first step in picking a sleeping bag is deciding upon a temperature rating. Just as there is no such thing as a four-season tent, there are no year-round sleeping bags. In general, for backpacking in the spring, summer, and fall, you will be best served by a bag rated to 20ºF and weighing less than 2.5 pounds. This is warm enough for chilly nights yet not sweltering when opened up like a blanket. If the temps really drop, you can augment the rating by wearing additional clothing.

Temperature ratings are highly subjective since many factors affect them, including your metabolism, level of fatigue, and thermal efficiency of your sleeping pad. Mainstream sleeping bag manufacturers now use a range system adopted in Europe with three ratings on the tag: a Comfort Limit at which most women are comfortable, a Lower Limit at which most men are comfortable, and an Extreme Rating, which is the lowest a woman might survive the night. Many ultralight sleeping bags from boutique companies use a rating closer to Extreme, so beware extravagant claims.

As for insulation material, high-grade goose down is still the first choice. A sleeping bag with 800-plus fill power down is significantly lighter and more compressible than any alternatives. If price is a prime consideration, then opting for 650-plus fill down won't mean a huge weight increase in a three-season bag but becomes very noticeable in winter bags. With a quality tent and a good stuff sack (see page 16), keeping down bags dry is not that difficult in all but the most extreme conditions.

If you will be backpacking in notoriously wet regions, particularly when using single-wall tents or tarps, then synthetic insulation can be a better option. The best of the modern synthetics rival 650-plus fill down for weight, bulk, and cost but not longevity or comfort on warmer nights. The inexpensive synthetic bags offer mediocre performance and value, though they beat the pants off anything we had three decades ago. By the way, people who

Left to right: 1. This ultralight mummy filled with high-quality down gives the best weight to warmth ratio. 2. For maximum weight savings, this semi-rectangular bag has no bottom; it attaches to a pad for insulation from the ground. 3. A wearable sleeping bag has armholes and a leg opening with a drawcord so you can perform camp chores. 4. For wet weather camping, it is wise to use a synthetic-filled sleeping bag—the best ones are now starting to rival down for minimal weight and bulk.

claim "warm when wet" have obviously never slept in one; "tolerably uncomfortable" is a more accurate description, so it behooves you to keep any sleeping bag dry.

Shell fabrics comprise a major portion of total bag weight and compressibility. Since durability is pretty much a nonissue, go with the lightest fabrics you can afford. Generally, microfiber nylons deliver the best performance. However, if you will spend a lot of time camping at or near below-freezing temperatures, a waterproof/breathable outer shell can help minimize condensation problems.

Mummy-style sleeping bags that have a hood and a tapered shape offer the best thermal efficiency. However, bags that are too tight or with partial-length zippers can prevent a good night's sleep; a few extra ounces will make life better. When camping mostly in above-freezing conditions, semi-rectangular bags without a hood offer great comfort.

Many hikers underestimate the importance of their pad to a good night's sleep. When they shiver through a cold night, the sleeping bag is often blamed when the real culprit is the inadequate pad. Like the walls of your home, pads are rated with an R-value. Anything less than an R-value of 2 is completely inadequate for cold ground and ensures a night of suffering even with a winter bag. Lesser ratings can be fine for hot weather, but you need at least an R-5 pad for sleeping on snow.

Having spent far too many a night on closed-cell foam pads, I cannot recommend them to anyone without masochist tendencies (or alpinists, same thing). Similarly, three-quarter-length pads sound good for reducing weight in theory but often equate to more tossing and turning during the night. Sleeping pads are

Left to right: 1. A good self-inflating pad offers comfort, warmth, and convenience. 2. Although a down-filled air mattress takes longer to inflate, it is incredibly comfortable and compact when rolled. 3. This high-end air mattress requires a lot of puffing but is lighter and more compact than other pads. 4. A hybrid between a closed-cell and self-inflating pad provides reasonable comfort and good durability. 5. This folding closed-cell pad has dimples to provide a bit more cushioning from hard ground; it's lightweight and inexpensive. Simply lay it out and go to bed.

an area where you can go silly light and hurt yourself or carry a few extra ounces and get a great sleep. Having paid my dues, I am now willing to carry a tad more for a minimum of 1.5 inches over my full length.

Your sleeping bag should come with a storage sack (use it) and a stuff sack (toss it). Do yourself a favor and purchase a silnylon waterproof stuff sack that has sealed seams and a roll-top closure; this is lighter and gives better protection. Even if you have a bulky sleeping bag, I don't recommend compression stuff sacks that use stamps because they are heavy, complicated, and don't make much of a difference.

For hot weather, you might consider using a sleeping bag liner made of cotton or silk. These keep your bag clean and can be used alone when it's sweltering. You can also augment the warmth of your sleeping bag with thermal liners that can boost the rating by 10 to 20ºF.

PACKS

Of the Big Three, we cover packs last because your prior decisions affect this one. With a lighter and more compact tent and sleeping bag, you can get away with a smaller and less supportive pack—at least for some trips. If you will be carrying climbing gear into the Cirque of the Towers or a large format camera into the Teton wilderness (guilty as charged), then a more substantial pack is needed.

The starting point for pack selection is volume because too small is frustrating and too large means you often bring the kitchen sink. Most people will find that a 4,000-cubic-inch pack has sufficient vol-

For fast and light trips, a good no-frills pack carries all of your gear with minimal weight and still has features you need. On longer trips, or when extra gear is required, a large internal-frame pack carries heavier loads comfortably; this one (right) has an outer pocket that detaches to become a daypack.

ume for extended weekend backpacking trips (two to three nights out). Those going Spartan might get by with 3,000 cubic inches, while those with bulkier gear may need as much as 6,000 cubic inches.

Volume dictates the amount of support required, though it is better to err on the side of more. Packs with a minimal frame may only weigh 2 pounds but can lead to sore shoulders and hips for all but the most hard-core ultralight backpackers. On the other hand, many over-built packs weigh 6 to 8 pounds

Even a frameless pack needs contoured shoulder straps and good ventilation for comfort (note the hip belt pocket on the red pack, a tremendously useful feature). The best internal-frame packs are fully customizable so you can dial in the fit for maximum comfort.

and ensure a tortoise-like pace. Somewhere in the region of 3 to 4 pounds is likely a good choice for many backpackers.

External-frame packs have gone the way of dinosaurs, though they are still the best choice for carrying 80-plus-pound loads. At the opposite extreme, frameless packs that rely on the sleeping pad for "support" are all the rage in the ultralight community. However, frameless packs require a parsimonious attitude that takes a lot of fun out of backpacking.

Internal-frame packs run the gamut from clean and elegant to complex monstrosities designed by the marketing department instead of users. If possible, try packs on in the shop with the appropriate weight inside and wear it around for at least a half hour to notice the subtle pressure points. Be sure to have the salesperson show you how to make all the fit adjustments so you can make tweaks on the trail.

When looking at backpacks, pay attention to the little things that get used a lot. For me, hip belt pockets are essential to carry items I want during the day, yet I have largely given up on hydration bladders so that feature is unimportant; your preferences may vary. If you like to bushwhack, avoid mesh side pockets that snag on every branch. Packs with dark interiors become black holes that make finding gear needlessly difficult; light-colored fabric really helps.

Keeping your gear dry while hiking in the rain is a bit of an art. For the most part, pack covers are rather heavy, flap in the wind, snag on bushes, and still don't work well due to condensation and perspiration from your back. A more reliable system is to use a pack liner, either purpose-built with sealed seams or a white compactor trash bag, and double-bag critical items like sleeping bag and warm clothes. This also protects from accidental submersion during a stream crossing, as well as leaky fuel bottles or hydration bladders.

ACCESSORIES

Right at the top of your list of essential accessories should be a map and compass. As a certified gear-head with all the gadgets, I can assure you I still carry the basic navigation tools even if I have my smart-phone and GPS receiver. Batteries die, electronics fail, cell signals don't reach when you need them. But a good compass and a map of the area will always get you through.

A good compass has built-in declination adjustment to compensate for magnetic north, a sighting mirror for accurate readings, and a long baseplate for working on maps.

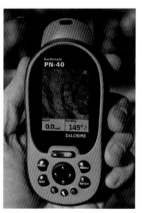

Nobody *needs* a GPS receiver to go backpacking. These high-tech gadgets are a nice luxury that

The best GPS receivers have large color displays, barometric altimeters, and high-quality topographic maps available for download. Be aware that some models with touch screens are virtually unreadable in direct sunlight, rendering them almost useless for backpacking.

can help in certain circumstances. Purchasing a GPS unit before you have mastered the art of navigation with map and compass is foolish.

Certainly on overnight trips, a headlamp is essential to help with chores. Even on day trips, it is wise to carry a small headlamp in your pack since accidents do happen. The single most important feature of any headlamp is a locking switch that cannot accidentally turn on inside your pack. Beyond that, it's nice to have a dim broad beam for tasks and a bright narrow beam for spotting distant objects.

A good headlamp for backpacking is compact, rugged, waterproof, and has multiple beam settings. For day excursions, an ultra-compact emergency headlamp weighs virtually nothing, takes up almost no space in the pack, and can really save your hide when needed.

While outdoor shops offer an array of multitools, it's hard to beat the venerable Swiss Army knife for backpacking. Though I own an assortment

Which knife to carry is a matter of preference. At times, scissors, a small blade, and miniature screwdriver (inside the corkscrew) all come in handy. Yet the longer locking blade, wood saw, and Philips head screwdriver also have their advantages.

of multi-tools, I find that the little ones are toys and don't do anything well and the big ones can do a lot of things I don't need when hiking, and are too heavy.

Depending on whom you talk with, trekking poles are either an essential bit of kit or an unnecessary hassle. The pro-pole crowd points to increased support on tricky terrain, greater safety during river crossings, reduced stress on knees, and the option of using the poles for supporting a tent. The anti-pole hikers note the extra energy wasted, the annoying clicking noise, and the irony that ultralight hikers have less need for support.

Trekking poles offer additional support on rocky trails, but some hikers don't think they are worth the extra energy required to carry and use them. Stephen Gorman

If you choose to use poles, learn to use the straps properly by inserting your hand from below so that the wrist is supported. Be sure the grip is comfortable in bare hands, the strap is padded, and the carbide tips are replaceable. Unless you have money to burn, features like shock absorbers and carbon fiber shafts aren't needed.

While some might consider an umbrella frivolous, there are two climates where they are worth their weight in gold. If you are hiking out in the open

A trekking umbrella is designed to hold its shape in strong wind and is made from silnylon to save weight. Good trekking poles (right) collapse to less than 20 inches long and extend to over 47 inches; the small trekking basket will not catch on underbrush and provides flotation in soft sand.

on hot days, the shade from an umbrella is far cooler than that offered by a hat. When backpacking in persistent rain without much wind, an umbrella is more comfortable than wearing a hood, keeps you and your gear drier, and lets you hear better.

Sunglasses are essential protection for your eyes both from UV light and wind. Although you can get by with fashion shades meant for driving, the best option for backpacking, particularly if you go above tree line, are models that wrap around the face.

Good outdoor sunglasses can adapt to variable lighting conditions, either by changing the lenses (top) or by using photochromic lenses that darken in bright light.

Chapter Three
Clothing

While the gear in your pack relates to your comfort in camp, it's the clothes on your back that affect comfort on the trail. Rather than thinking of clothes as individual items, it is better to look at clothing systems for different environmental conditions.

FOOTWEAR SYSTEMS

Where the rubber hits the trail can have a lot to do with a successful backpacking trip. With proper selection, you'll barely notice what is on your feet and focus on the experience. However, inadequate footwear, improper fit, or ill-suited socks can quickly turn a great hike into huge misery.

Hiking shoes differ from trail runners in the stiffness of the midsole. Although a bit heavier, the stiffer flex provides a more solid platform when walking on rough trails, and it helps prevent bruising the bottom of the feet from stepping on sharp rocks. Trail running shoes tend to be lighter, which saves energy, and more flexible, which causes fatigue; their primary advantage is superior breathability and faster drying time after getting wet.

Both hiking and trail running shoes are available with waterproof/breathable linings, but this option

Trail running shoes (right) are lightweight but offer minimal protection for your feet. Good hiking shoes (left) are a better option for backpacking because they generally offer more support and superior traction. When carrying a heavier pack through rugged terrain, especially if there is mud and snow, good medium-weight backpacking boots (top) are worth the extra weight.

costs more, adds weight, makes them hot, and keeps your feet wet if water comes in over the ankles; don't bother unless you plan to wear gaiters.

Despite what many people think, lightweight hiking boots do not provide any ankle support. These are essentially over-the-ankle shoes that help keep dirt and water away from your socks. Light hikers are a good choice both for day hikes and short backpacking trips, particularly if wet conditions are anticipated. Better models have waterproof/breathable linings and relatively few seams for greater durability.

Medium-weight backpacking boots offer extra protection, support, and durability for more rugged terrain and heavier loads. These are a good choice for trekking in remote areas where an injury can have real consequences.

If you are carrying a heavy pack over rugged terrain that may lack trails, heavy-duty backpacking boots are a good choice. Generally made from full-grain leather with few seams, these boots are also suitable for general mountaineering with crampons.

Frequently, the footbeds provided with new hiking boots are made from cheap foam that flattens quickly. Many backpackers will benefit from aftermarket footbeds that cradle the foot and distribute pressure more evenly. These can enhance ankle support and alleviate some blister problems, though some combinations can move blisters to a different spot.

One item you definitely do not want to skimp on is hiking socks; they have improved greatly in recent years. Good quality socks carefully blend wool and other materials to absorb perspiration and reduce friction. If you have trouble with blisters, try different socks before replacing boots.

A part of the footwear system that is often overlooked, foot ointments can go a long way toward preventing blisters. These nongreasy formulas, such as Hydropel, rubbed onto your feet help transport moisture away from the skin and reduce friction.

With lightweight boots and shoes, a single pair of high-quality wool blend socks is the best option. Most backpackers wearing heavier boots are more comfortable with two pairs of socks. The inner pair (top) is a light or a synthetic material that wicks moisture away from the foot. The outer pair (bottom) is a heavier wool and synthetic blend, providing moisture absorption and comfort. The two pairs move against each other instead of rubbing against your feet. Stephen Gorman

Knee-length gaiters can be very useful when there is still snow in the backcountry and when bushwhacking while wearing shorts. Select a model with waterproof fabric below the ankle and breathable fabric above. A front opening is more convenient than side or rear, and neoprene or cable instep straps last much longer than string.

HOT-WEATHER SYSTEM

Your choice of clothing for hiking in hot weather will depend on the region of the country and the time of year. Your first inclination may be to wear shorts and a short-sleeved shirt, and in many places this may indeed be excellent. However, in areas where tick-borne diseases are a problem, it is wise to wear long pants and a long-sleeved shirt. Similarly, when hiking in the desert during summer months, the extra sun protection of long clothing is prudent.

When selecting shorts for backpacking, examine the waist region for seams and rivets that create pressure points underneath a hip belt. Also be sure there are no rough seams around the inner thigh that will chafe. Somewhat baggy shorts offer good airflow without snagging on brush. Nylon fabric is faster drying and more durable than cotton. Many hikers opt for convertible pants with legs that zip off to become shorts.

While tempting, cotton T-shirts are lousy for backpacking because they get soaked with sweat and chafe your skin. For greater comfort, select a loose-fitting T-shirt made from polyester knit since it offers good airflow and fast drying while protecting your shoulders from the sun. Women may also wish to wear a sports bra with mesh ventilation, but check for seams that will chafe or create pressure points under shoulder straps.

The best option for hiking in hot weather is loose-fitting, long-sleeved shirts and pants made of nylon fabric. If it's also bug season, clothing with an insect shield treatment will greatly improve your comfort. Be sure to wear a hat with a full brim to keep sun off your face, neck, and ears (baseball caps don't cut it).

In areas where ticks, mosquitoes, and blackflies are a problem, your best option is to wear long clothing, tuck your pants into your socks, wear light colors so you can see ticks more easily, and even wear a head net if the bugs are really bad. You might also consider treating your hiking clothes with an insect repellent called permethrin to reduce the need for using bug sprays and lotions on your skin. Pre-treated insect repellant clothing lasts about fifty washings before losing efficacy. Or you can purchase permethrin spray and treat your own clothing, which lasts about five washings.

Particularly where Lyme disease is prevalent, be sure to treat your hiking socks (and short gaiters if you wear them) with permethrin too.

Hiking pants, whether convertible or not, should have a gusseted crotch and articulated knees for maximum freedom of movement. Stretch nylon is the best fabric option though you may also desire mesh side vents for increased airflow. While knit fabrics are a good choice for T-shirts, long-sleeve hiking shirts should be woven synthetic to prevent mosquitoes biting through the material.

Desert hikers don't have to deal with bugs; instead, they have the oppressive sun. Long clothing is advisable, preferably white, though you may find cotton is cooler than synthetics. These days, some clothing has ratings for sun protection, and it is worthwhile looking for SPF 50 on the hangtag.

Since wearing long pants reduces ventilation, you may experience chafing of the inner thighs. Synthetic boxer shorts may be one solution because they are longer than briefs and dry quickly. Another possibility is compression undershorts (like bike shorts without the padding) that give a smooth sliding surface. You also might try anti-chafing lubricants, such as Body Glide, to reduce friction.

Hats are also an important component of a hot-weather clothing system. While baseball caps and mesh running hats make a fashion statement, they also say you don't care about sun protection. Smart hikers wear hats with full brims that protect the ears and neck. Should you be forced to wear mosquito netting to keep bloodsuckers at bay, a full-brim hat increases comfort. In particularly brutal sun, you may even wish to use an umbrella for shade.

COOL-WEATHER SYSTEM

When hiking in the spring, fall, or at high altitudes, you will need a versatile layering system that can quickly

White, medium-weight synthetic tops keep you cool in the sun and dry quickly. High-quality, medium-weight merino wool underwear (center) is comfortable next to the skin and helps regulate temperature. For the coldest conditions, heavyweight synthetic (left) can be worn over lighter layers.

adjust to the conditions. And even though the days may be sweltering in the desert or high mountains, the nights are often downright chilly, so extra layers should be at hand.

For base layers, you will probably find medium-weight long underwear the most useful because it wicks moisture well, provides some but not too much warmth, and works well alone and in combination with other layers. Modern synthetics deliver the best performance because the fabrics dry quickly, are comfortable next to the skin, and the better versions no longer suffer problems with odor retention. Merino wool has made a resurgence in recent years because it is relatively warm when wet, naturally odor resistant, and superior processing has eliminated most of the scratchiness.

There are a gazillion options for mid-layer tops that provide some insulation, block wind, and resist moisture. Among the most popular choices is a windshirt with wicking polyester knit lining; this works well on its own and under other layers since it slides easily. Softshells made with stretch woven fabrics provide greater abrasion resistance but are a bit heavier and bulkier in the pack. Though less weather resistant, fleece tops also make great mid-layers due to good warmth and breathability. So far, windproof fleece is unsatisfactory for the backcountry due to weight, bulk, and slow drying time.

For your legs, it's hard to beat a good pair of soft-

The combination of mid-weight synthetic with a windshell (left) is superb as both a mid-layer and an outershell. Stretch softshell jackets are great outer layers on cold days when you are active; underarm zippers allow more ventilation when working hard.

shell pants: They are rugged, allow great freedom of movement, provide moderate warmth, resist wind, and repel water. Features you want include a thigh pocket, zippered gussets on the lower leg, and instep patches.

There are lots of choices too for insulating outer layers. As with sleeping bags, down offers maximum warmth with minimum weight and bulk. However, synthetic-insulated tops are also excellent because you can toss them on over wet clothes and stay warm as things dry. In milder conditions, a vest may be all you need when combined with other layers. But if colder weather is anticipated, you will appreciate a nice sweater or jacket.

When bugs are not a concern, good nylon hiking shorts are a plea-sure to wear. Pants made for backpacking (right) are made with rugged, quick-drying fabric and a waist that will not create pressure points underneath a hip belt. In colder weather, stretch softshell mountaineering pants (center) provide durability, wind and water resistance, and great freedom of movement. Windpants with a mid-weight synthetic lining and full-length side zippers (left) can be easily donned over pants or shorts as part of a layering system.

A stocking hat and lightweight gloves play a vital role in staying warm. Although the oft-heard claim that 90 percent of your heat is lost through your head is utter nonsense, a fleece or wool hat does help you

A high-quality down vest (right) offers a tremendous warmth-to-weight ratio and takes up little space in the pack. A favorite layer for many alpinists, a synthetic-insulated jacket (center) blocks the wind better than fleece, is more compact when stuffed, and dries very quickly. If conditions are dry, an ultralight down sweater (left) is a remarkably comfortable insulation layer.

effectively regulate body temperature. Thin fleece gloves provide just enough warmth without sacrificing dexterity, are reasonably durable, and dry quickly.

STORM SYSTEM

The level of storm protection you need depends greatly upon where and when you go backpacking. Certainly the needs of those in the Pacific Northwest differ from those in the Rockies. And springtime in New England can be a soggy experience while fall seldom sees much inclement weather.

A basic windshirt made from ultralight nylon (front) can be a great complement to a heavier rainshell. In chilly weather, a hooded windshell made with a Windstopper laminate (upper right) is ideal for high aerobic output. For complete rain protection, a light parka with a waterproof/breathable laminate and no lining (upper center) offers a good compromise of minimum weight and bulk. When durability counts, a mountain shell made with a three-ply waterproof/breathable fabric (upper left) gives the greatest longevity.

In relatively dry climates, storm protection is something brought out infrequently and often put away after the thunderstorm passes, thus lightweight and compactness are important. Often it is used more as a windshell than a rainshell, so breathability is also a consideration.

In damper climes with high humidity, breathability

is a relative term since there is only so much any fabric can do; excellent ventilation is key. Understand that you *will* get wet in some conditions, even with the very best shells available, because of condensation rather than leaking fabric—plan accordingly. For some trips, you may wear the jacket and pants all day long, so you will probably want a bit more durability. Ponchos are only passable in the most benign places where the wind doesn't blow and the temperatures are warm; otherwise, they are a prescription for misery.

Among the most essential features of a good stormshell is a well-designed hood that allows peripheral vision, keeps glasses dry, and does not channel water inside. Mesh-lined pockets double as vents, but these often must be closed when it's really dumping, so underarm zippers are still desirable. Smarter designs have a pocket that also doubles as a stuff sack.

Storm pants should be simple but not too simple. Forget any storm pants that require removing boots to put on and take off. Full-length side zippers will leak, so they are only recommended for winter use when you need to take pants off while wearing skis or crampons. Because your pack's hip belt tends to push them down, pants need a good belt or waist closure that doesn't create pressure points (e.g., no cordlocks).

When hiking in all-day drizzle, you may wish to use a rain hat with a full brim, or an umbrella, instead of your jacket's hood. This allows you to hear much better and helps prevent overheating when working hard.

Chapter Four

Kitchen and Food

The Romans knew that an army marches on its stomach. Backpackers too know that food fuels their hikes. But more than that, food sets the mood and tenor of your trips. Some decide to go hardcore and eat flavorless yet easy-to-prepare meals. Others prefer to enjoy delectable treats during the day and a four-course gourmet repast accompanied by adult beverages at dinner.

STOVES

Gather a dozen backpackers together and it's almost certain the topic of conversation will turn to stoves. For whatever reason, many backpackers have a stove fetish and end up with a collection. The primary fuel options are butane, white gas, and alcohol, with some stoves capable of burning multiple fuels.

With proper understanding of use and limitations, the majority of backpackers will be well served by stoves that use screw-on butane (actually either isobutane or a butane/propane blend) cartridges. These are generally easy to operate and reliable; however, the basic models do struggle in cold weather. More sophisticated stoves use inverted canisters and preheating to improve performance in the cold.

In cold weather, a white gas stove with a pump inside the fuel bottle (rear) is the most reliable option; efficiency can be increased further with high-performance aluminum pots. In warmer weather, butane stoves (center) offer the greatest convenience and are compact enough to fit inside the cookset. Some stoves are designed to use either white gas or butane (front); with an integrated windscreen and pots designed to capture heat, this is a good system for any weather.

White gas stoves have long been the preferred option for backpacking due to efficiency as well as the availability and affordability of fuel. Though I have owned many, these days I seldom use white gas stoves, even in the winter, because of the convenience and safety of butane. Once you learn a particular stove's quirks and how to maintain it, white gas stoves do crank out a lot of heat no matter the temperature and at low altitude. If you will be cooking for more than two or three people, white gas stoves are likely your best option.

Alcohol stoves are popular among ultralight backpackers because the stoves are simple and light; long-distance hikers appreciate the ready availability of ethanol and methanol. However, these stoves are slow to boil water, perform poorly in wind or cold temperatures, seldom have heat control, and the fuel burns with an invisible flame when accidentally spilled.

Stoves that integrate with pots have increased in popularity though they are not necessarily superior to well-chosen separate components. When picking a butane or white gas stove, be sure that the pot supports are sheet metal with teeth instead of round rods since pots are less likely to slide off accidentally.

No matter the stove and cookset, a vital component is an effective windscreen. It is best to purchase one designed for the stove since it can also increase efficiency. Improvised windscreens can work, but

Eating out of the pot isn't always an option, so a collapsible bowl can simplify mealtime. An aluminum knife, fork, and spoon can be lighter and more durable than plastic versions. Leave the antique Sierra cup at home and carry a modern insulated mug that won't spill and will keep your drink warm.

care must be taken to prevent overheating the fuel tank on some stoves to prevent an explosion.

COOK GEAR

Pots and a windscreen should be considered an integral part of your cooking system. Proper selection can significantly increase fuel efficiency, especially when cooking in the wind. Backpacking pots are made either from aluminum, stainless steel, or titanium.

The best pots are aluminum with a hard anodized coating for durability and ease of cleanup. Look for a textured base to help prevent dinner sliding onto the ground. Stainless steel pots can take more abuse than other materials, but that factor isn't worth the extra weight. Titanium is great for ultralight fetishists but has a poor cost-benefit ratio.

Many backpackers prefer the convenience of meals that rehydrate in their packaging. If you go with this scheme, then you only need a single pot for boiling water and a pot cozy to keep things warm as they rehydrate. On the other hand, if you prefer making a full-blown meal, then at least one additional pot is required. The fancier your dining, then the more extensive your kitchen requirements.

All but the ultralight hardcores will want a nice insulated cup, a spoon, and possibly a bowl. A simple spice kit can greatly improve meals; a mini grater and some Parmesan cheese can make a huge difference.

Some of us won't be caught dead without good coffee in the morning, preferably fresh ground. While a French press or stovetop espresso maker suits some, cleanup is a hassle. For great taste with easy cleanup and minimal bulk and weight, the best option is a coffee filter.

Backpackers often find themselves in bear country as well the home of many other critters. Depending on where you travel, precautions are often needed to protect your food from marauders. Some areas require bear canisters, while others permit hanging food (see chapter 8). Shelters in some places have annoying mice or raccoons that are smarter than many people, so elaborate precautions may be necessary.

BACKPACKING FOOD

Since food is one of the heaviest stuff sacks in your pack, the temptation may be to cut back—potentially a big mistake. Insufficient calories will leave you sluggish and tired, which can contribute to accidents and possibly even put you in a dangerous situation. A starvation diet results in muscle loss too, so it's a poor method for losing body fat.

Many factors affect your caloric needs, including weight, metabolism, and difficulty of the hike. For a ballpark estimate of daily requirement when back-

Freeze-dried food is the lightest option out there for backpackers, but it can also be the most expensive. Stephen Gorman

packing in the mountains, multiply your weight in pounds times 22. Thus a person weighing 120 pounds needs about 2,640 calories while a 200-pounder needs 4,400 calories. On easy days, you can do well with less, but on long, hard days even that amount will leave you hungry.

Most of the freeze-dried meals sold in outdoor shops that supposedly have "two servings" barely have enough calories for a single hungry hiker (dinners often allow just 300 to 400 calories per person). To make matters worse, they are expensive, the flavors are bland, and the texture is best described as lumpy mush. On the plus side, they are fast and easy.

Fortunately, there are many good options for trail foods from small specialty companies (e.g., PackIt Gourmet) that combine freeze-dried and dehydrated foods to produce superior recipes. You can also do well by shopping at supermarkets and natural grocers for "instant" meals. And many backpackers prepare meals at home by drying foods in a dehydrator or oven.

On shorter trips where weight may be less of a concern, hydrated foods in sturdy foil packages (such as tuna and Indian meals) are a great way to supplement instant rice, couscous, or pasta. You can boost the calories and flavor of many meals by adding nuts, hard cheese, or salami; these all keep for a week or more on the trail. Also, bring some dried herbs in small bags and individual packets of hot sauce and honey to make the bland more interesting.

You can reduce weight and bulk, plus simplify life considerably, by repackaging meals into zip-lock bags. It helps tremendously at the end of a long day to just pull out a meal with all the pertinent information (water required, cook time) on the outside and get'er done.

The most convenient backpacking meals are packaged in food-grade plastic bags (either prepackaged or do-it-yourself freezer bags); simply add boiling water, wrap the meal with insulation, and wait. When ready, just eat out of the bag. These one-bag meals save fuel since there is no simmering, no pots to clean, and extra hot water can be used for drinks.

If you don't mind a little after-dinner cleanup, there are also many excellent one-pot meal possibilities; this is often the best option with groups. Rather than simmering the entire time, save fuel by boiling water, adding your ingredients, then shutting off the stove and waiting a bit longer than normal. For tender food, start rehydrating with cold water as soon as you get to camp, then set up your tent and attend to other chores before cooking.

Another option is to do a hybrid meal where the instant rice or couscous rehydrates in a freezer bag while you cook up a sauce with the yummy protein and fats. This doesn't work with pasta unless it has been precooked.

There is a lot to be said for making the first dinner of your backpacking trip an amazing one. It's easy to keep many vegetables fresh for a day, and you can even freeze something like a steak and carry it wrapped inside your sleeping bag. This sets a great tone for the rest of your trip and, if there are leftovers, makes for a good breakfast too.

Since you want to break camp and get on the trail quickly in the morning, breakfasts should be fast and easy. Don't bother with things like pancakes and instead opt for oatmeal and granola. However, don't deny yourself good coffee or tea since that helps with your hydration and bowel movements.

When backpacking with a small group (two to four people), it is best to eat communally but find out about likes, dislikes, and allergies ahead of time; larger groups should break up into cook teams. It is also a good idea to make one person (preferably the most skilled) the designated cook; they get their tent pitched by the others.

Lunches and snacks tend to be individual affairs with some sharing. There is no need to eat energy bars or gels since real food is just as effective and a lot tastier. Make your own trail mix by going to stores with bulk bins and picking the things you like. Tortillas are the best sandwich bread since they hold up well on the trail and can be used for a wide range of options.

For much more detailed information on back-country eating, food to bring, and campsite cooking, check out the *Backpacker Magazine* companion guide *Campsite Cooking* for details.

Chapter Five
Water

When backpacking, we often visit pristine areas that have untainted water sources. However, in many regions it is best to err on the side of caution and treat your drinking water to prevent illness from giardia, cryptosporidium, and other nasties.

Water treatment can be performed by boiling, filtration, or chemical methods. In extreme cases of badly contaminated water, multiple methods may be required though this is seldom the case when backpacking.

Beware! Tempting as it might be to dip your water bottle into a clear mountain stream, risking a bout with giardia is not worth it.

Stephen Gorman

Since boiling kills all potential pathogens, the water used for cooking meals and hot drinks is safe. You may have heard it takes five to ten minutes of boiling, but this is a waste of fuel and not needed; once water reaches a roiling boil (even at high altitude), all microorganisms are destroyed. Boiled water can be allowed to cool for drinking, but it has a flat, metallic taste.

Water filters have improved in recent years, making them faster, smaller, lighter, and less finicky. Having struggled with many different models in the past, I had almost given up on filters entirely. But modern pump filters offer fast delivery of clean water without any taste issues. The new gravity-feed filters are great for watering larger groups since they require almost no work. However, filters are ineffective against viruses, so they should not be relied on in Third World countries. And because freezing can cause filters to crack, they are not recommended in the winter.

While once very popular, iodine treatment methods are no longer recommended due to numerous problems, including inefficacy against crypto. The nasty taste can be alleviated by adding vitamin C (such as in sport drinks); however, if this is done too soon, then the water is unsafe. Very cold water requires a higher dosage or much longer wait than the standard thirty minutes. Finally, the iodine tablets have a short shelf life (three months) once the bottle is opened.

Newer water filters that can convert to gravity-feed (rear) are a good choice for individuals and groups. When supplying water for just one or two people, a water bottle with integrated UV-C light (front) is a very fast and convenient method.

A better alternative is chlorine dioxide treatment, which imparts minimal taste. Though the name sounds similar, this is chemically very different from the chlorine found in bleach (not recommended). Chlorine dioxide still takes fifteen to thirty minutes depending on water temperature (four hours in severe cases), and mixing the liquids is a nuisance. The chlorine dioxide pills work well but are a bit costly; they are a good backup for other methods.

The newest method of water treatment, ultraviolet light, is now my favorite. It only takes two minutes to kill the nasties in clear water (longer if it's cloudy), so you can enjoy safe, fresh water when you stop at a stream. The drawback to UV-C is the reliance on batteries, and it only works with a liter at a time, which may be impractical for larger groups.

WATER TREATMENT TIPS

Whatever the treatment method, start with the best water source possible. Rather than the outlet of a pond, try to use the inlet where the water is fresher or out in the middle where things have had a chance to settle out. Get as near the source as possible, such as where a stream emerges from the ground or snowbank. Be aware of what may be upstream, farms and "wilderness" with grazing livestock in particular.

If there is a lot of sediment in the water, it is a good idea to prefilter by pouring through a fresh coffee filter. This keeps filters from clogging and helps chemical treatments work faster. Water with a great deal of fine sediment can be left in a container overnight to settle out, but be sure you don't stir it up when decanting the good water.

No matter which methods you use for treating water, they are all for naught if you are not careful about hygiene while on the trail. Good hygiene starts with keeping fingernails short and cleaning your hands after going to the bathroom. Thankfully, this is easy due to the availability of hand sanitizer in small containers. Less obvious sources of contamination include washing dishes or brushing teeth with contaminated water and even shaking hands with other hikers. Also pay attention that dirty water does not contaminate your treated water.

Ultimately, deciding whether water needs to be treated is a value judgment based on your location and your risk tolerance. Nothing in the water will kill you if it isn't treated; at worst we are talking about a bad case of gastric distress. However, dehydration can lead to disorientation and even heat stroke, which definitely can kill you and quickly. Don't be foolish and forego drinking water from a stream or lake if you or your hiking partner is overheating.

Chapter Six
Trip Planning

Whether an overnight trip or a multiweek journey, you will reap the greatest rewards by preparing for your adventure. Remember the five P's: Proper Planning Prevents Poor Performance.

We have already covered the basics of equipment and food choices. The next part of your trip preparation involves deciding who will be joining you, where and when you will go. This will allow you to fine-tune your gear and food selection, develop a realistic timeline, and anticipate potential problems. For an advanced discussion on these topics, see my book *Climbing: Expedition Planning* (2003).

Partnering up is easy if your soul mate also enjoys backpacking and has a similar level of fitness. But it gets more complicated if you have different visions about goals and degrees of comfort. Do everyone a favor and sort out potential issues ahead of time. Unrealistic expectations have led to many a nightmarish trip.

Once you have your partner(s) lined up, or decide to go it alone, pull out the guidebooks (or go to www.backpacker.com/destinations) and pick a trail. You'll quickly learn that not all miles are created equal, so judging by distance alone can leave you coming up short. In addition to trail descriptions, better guidebooks will include time estimates, elevation gain and loss, and warnings about less obvious hazards. If you are going into less-traveled areas, you may have to glean this information from topo maps or even Google Earth.

Don't scoff at the value of advance research. For example, if you go to the Bugaboos in British Columbia and don't know about the voracious porcupines that like to eat the radiator hoses on cars, your great trip can end on a huge sour note. You're also in for a rude awakening if you think you can just show up and get a permit for the Mt. Whitney Trail in summer without a reservation.

It is also wise to note contact information for ranger offices, permit requirements, and emergency numbers. Many areas have specific rules about traveling in bear country, and what is fine in one area may not be allowed in others.

Find out when hunting season starts and ends. If you are out on the trails during this time, it is wise to add some blaze orange to your clothing or pack. Avoid wearing white because a glimpse through the trees can resemble the flash of a deer's tail.

Part of your research should include prevailing weather patterns for your destination, especially if it's several states away. It helps to know that a snowstorm is a real possibility in August when hiking in Colorado's high country. As your departure date gets closer, start following the weather on the Internet.

Trail running is a great way to train for backpacking. Being in good shape will greatly enhance your wilderness experience.

Stephen Gorman

These days, "surprise" storms are exceedingly rare, and getting caught unprepared is foolish.

Pick realistic goals and save the ambitious projects for when you have the experience and fitness to pull them off. Especially before doing a mega-trip, it is wise to do a couple of mini shakedown trips to evaluate your gear, your partners, and your own readiness. A big trip may quickly be cut short by a pair of ill-fitting boots or participants who bite off more than they can chew.

Some teams will divide communal gear among themselves for equal weight distribution (for example, one person carrying the tent body and another the poles and fly). A better method is for one to carry the complete tent and the other to carry the complete kitchen; if they somehow get separated, each can survive the night reasonably well off.

Splitting group weight evenly is also unfair if one person has significantly less lean muscle mass than the rest of the group (women have more body fat than men so total weight is inaccurate). To avoid "domestic moments," the stronger person should shoulder more group gear and the heavier pack.

One ultimate truth of backpacking: The fitter you are, the more enjoyable the experience. If you are heading off on a multiday trip and are badly out of shape compared to other people in the group, it's likely to be an unpleasant experience. It's far better to arrive in camp pleasantly tired than feeling like you just survived a death march. Give yourself a few months with a proper conditioning program before any major excursions.

PLANNING YOUR PACK

The little things can add up to make a big difference. If you start out with a good organization system, life out on the trail will be simpler and more pleasant. For example, it helps to keep cook gear together so you aren't always looking for a lighter. And there is no point in pulling out your sleeping bag until the tent is set up.

Rather than put all your food in one big bag, it is better to divide it into smaller sacks for breakfast (and morning drinks), midday (lunch, snacks, and drink mixes), and dinner. This makes it easy to always have trail food handy since it can be atop everything else.

The next step of pack planning is eliminating redundancy. Whenever possible, you want to carry gear that serves multiple functions. Think: Less is more. Pay attention to what you use, and especially what you don't use, on trips and figure out what can be eliminated.

Instead of carrying large bottles of sunscreen and bug repellent, take just what you need in small vials. Food can often be repackaged to reduce garbage; be sure to bring the cooking instructions. Don't take the entire guidebook; photocopy the relevant pages and you'll save weight and bulk, and the book lasts longer. One pair of extra socks is good, but two is excessive for most trips. Spare underwear, sleeping bag liners, and emergency blankets are just deadweight.

When deciding what to cut, think twice about eliminating insulation and food. While ultralight fanatics and alpinists like to cut things to the bone, this can be a roll of the dice with serious consequences—pull it off and the admirers rave; when things go wrong, they howl about unpreparedness. Seldom will an extra fleece sweater and bit of food slow you down significantly; if they do, blame your physical fitness and not the gear.

Similarly, a first-aid and repair kit is something you will hopefully never need. But reducing it too much, or leaving it behind, can mean the difference between minor inconvenience and an aborted trip.

It really helps to have things you will need during the day near the top of your pack. Better yet, carry snacks in hip belt pockets and have your water bottle located so you can reach it without removing your pack.

After all that planning, it's time to load up your pack. As a rule of thumb, you want the heaviest items (generally food and water) in the center of your pack and close to your back for greatest load transfer to the hips and stability. Most people carry the sleeping bag inside the bottom of the pack with the tent just above. It is an exceptionally bad idea to carry tent poles on the outside of the pack—they will get lost. After the tent goes food and kitchen; if using a gas stove, keep the fuel below your food in case of leaks. Then clothing goes on top of the pack so you have quick access.

Chapter Seven
On the Trail

You've planned, you've packed, and you've arrived at the trailhead; now it's time to start walking. Not so fast! Before you head out, tell someone where you are going, what trails you are taking, and when you expect to return. Don't count on being able to call 911 on your cell phone or even get a satellite signal with an emergency locator. Some people leave itineraries on the dashboard of their car but, alas, that is also an invitation for robbery.

It is wise to get an early start so you have plenty of time for the day's agenda. This is especially important in the Rockies where afternoon thunderstorms often dash above-tree-line plans. Sometimes you may even wish to sleep at the trailhead if it is permitted.

Start out for your hike well fed and hydrated since this is "free" weight and may even save you from having to carry lunch. Also take the time to adjust your socks so there are no wrinkles and lace your boots up so they are snug in all the right places.

When putting on your pack, it is best to lift it by the grab handle between the shoulder straps. If the pack is heavy, slide it up so the bottom rests on the top of your thigh, then bend down and tuck one arm through a shoulder strap and stand up all the way. Hunch your shoulders to raise the pack up a bit, fasten the hip belt,

The time to consult the map is before you get lost. Dave Anderson

and adjust the buckle so the belt is snug. Often you will want to fiddle with the shoulder and stabilizer straps a bit so that there are no pressure points.

Once you begin hiking, maintain a strong, steady pace. At the end of the day, you will be less tired if you avoid intervals of hiking hard followed by catching your breath. Don't bother with techniques such as "rest steps" or "pressure breathing" because they don't really work. Just find a pace that you can keep up all day long and stick with it.

It is generally better to take frequent short breaks instead of occasional long stops. You'll find it is hard to get going after setting your pack down and allowing your muscles to cool. Use those short breaks to look around, eat some snacks, sip some water, and take some photos. As soon as you feel a chill, get going again.

Many backpackers have rued their decision to "tough it out" when they felt a hot spot on their feet. What could have been a simple five-minute stop to treat an impending blister instead becomes days of pain dealing with a full-blown raw spot.

You might be able to walk and chew gum at the same time. But don't try to hike and read a map, or hike and drink from a bottle, or hike and take a photo. Far too many accidents occurred when a moment's inattention caused a stumble or even walking off the trail! You should never be in such a hurry that you can't stop for a moment—leave that attitude in the city. Heck, even smell the roses.

Another good time to stop is at stream crossings. These can be an opportunity to rehydrate and refill your water bottles or bladders. On hot days, there is special pleasure in a quick soak of your feet. Even just submerging your wrists can help cool your body temperature.

The art of navigating in the backcountry revolves around never getting lost in the first place. Sounds blindingly obvious, but it's remarkable how many people cannot point to their location on a map once they leave the trailhead. Many seem to trudge along oblivious to the surroundings and barely cognizant of trail markings.

Smart backpackers keep a mental map of their approximate position as they hike. They confirm their location whenever they get to a trail junction or notable landmark. And they frequently look behind them because they know going in the reverse direction can look amazingly different. Unless you are going off trail through deep forest or above tree line in a whiteout, it isn't that hard to stay found. See the *Backpacker* companion book *Trailside Navigation* as a good introduction or *Advanced Outdoor Navigation* (FalconGuides) for a more in-depth discussion.

Keep an eye on time too so that you know well in advance if you are falling behind schedule. It is infinitely better to reach your campsite with an hour or two of daylight left. If it becomes apparent that you won't reach your destination when hoped, it may be better to start looking for an alternative camp.

TRAIL BEHAVIOR

How your group interacts can be harmonious if everyone has a positive attitude and reasonable expectations. Or the group can devolve to discord and bickering when people become selfish and unyielding. Trust me, the former is better.

There is often a tendency for the fittest hikers to go charging up the trail, leaving the rest of the group far behind. Aside from the greater risk of people getting lost, this can create resentment that dampens the trip for everyone. A smarter course of action is to load the speed demons up with more weight and hike at the pace of the slowest person. That way everyone gets their workout and arrives together.

With larger groups, it is a good idea to designate a lead person on the trail (not necessarily the group leader) and a sweep. The lead should keep at least one other person within sight. When you get to a trail junction, everyone waits until the sweep is visible and clearly knows the proper direction.

You have two basic choices when you encounter other trail users: You can be pleasant or you can be a jerk. The former will say "howdy" or comment on the weather; the latter will pass in cold silence oozing bad vibes. Even worse is the loud jerk who has long conversations, shouts to make echoes, or pollutes the wilderness with noise.

When you encounter other hikers on the trail, the uphill hiker has the right-of-way. If you are heading down, be polite and step aside unless they decide to take a breather. Before moving off trail though, do a quick check for poison ivy and sound footing (bad form to go splat while getting out of the way). If you come upon a slower party from behind, ask permission to pass, then hastily do so on the left.

It is generally best for larger groups to yield to smaller groups, but this too can depend on the situation. Don't clog the trail by hiking two abreast either, unless there is plenty of room to pass.

Mountain bikers on designated trails have as much a right to be there as you do. In theory, bikers are always supposed to yield to hikers; however, they have to pass you at some point. So anticipate this and be prepared to step aside when it's convenient. Since mountain bikes have a hard time getting started again on uphills, it is best to step out of their way before they reach you. If you encounter mountain bikers on a closed trail (and you are absolutely sure), don't hesitate to give them an earful!

If you encounter pack animals, either going up or downhill, always give the animal the right-of-way. When you step aside for horses, try to go on the downhill side of the trail because they will be less likely to bolt (things above them are often predators). However, yaks have a fondness for knocking hikers off trails, so go uphill of those beasts.

SINGING IN THE RAIN

There is no such thing as staying dry while backpacking all day in the rain! One way or another, you will get wet. The good news is that you can be perfectly comfortable even when a bit damp if you plan for it.

The problem is that when working hard while carrying a pack in high humidity, you are going to sweat. This is compounded by condensation that can form inside outer shells when warm, moist air hits cold fabric. Waterproof/breathable fabrics are a huge help, but even the best of them can only do so much. Opening up vents isn't a perfect solution either since water has a way of finding its way inside.

The trick to enjoying rainy weather is making the most of your gear. Dress with quick-drying layers next to your skin and perhaps a lightweight mid-layer. The key is to generate warmth from hiking so you don't need a lot of insulation. Fabrics such as Gore-Tex work best when they are cleaned using a washing machine and dryer to ensure water beads up and rolls off; heavily used shells may need a reapplication of the DWR outer coating. Unless in a driving downpour, keep your vents open and use a rain hat or an umbrella instead of a hood.

Since rocks and roots can be treacherously slick when wet, using hiking poles is an especially good idea in the rain. Adjust them relatively short though so water doesn't run down your sleeves. When there are puddles in the trail, it is best to walk through them because walking around does more damage.

Lightning storms should be taken very seriously, especially when there is less than thirty seconds between the flash and the thunder. Get down off an exposed ridge or summit immediately. Try to seek shelter among a low stand of trees—never the highest tree in the area—and keep the group spread out at least 100 feet apart. If you can't find trees, look for low ground among boulders and cower in a crouching position.

BATTLING BUGS

Biting bugs have always been a nuisance. But in this age of West Nile fever (mosquitoes) and Lyme disease (ticks), both seriously debilitating conditions, preventing bug bites has taken on a new urgency.

The old standby, DEET, is still the best bug repellent on the market and lasts for about four hours, although the 30 percent strength is all you need. So far, none of the herbal repellents have proven effective for more than an hour or two. And the electronic gizmos are a joke. When conditions are especially bad, a mosquito-proof head net worn over a wide-brim hat and long-sleeved clothing treated with permethrin are your best option.

When the ticks are bad in the summer, wear a long-sleeved shirt and long pants with gaiters or the legs tucked into your socks. Lighter-colored clothing makes it easier to spot ticks and will be cooler in the sun. Hike in the center of the trail and avoid tall grass and bushes. If you hike with a dog, be sure it has protection against ticks as well.

STREAM CROSSINGS

Crossing raging creeks and swollen rivers is argu-

The safest way to cross a stream is usually one person at a time while using a pair of trekking poles. Stephen Gorman

ably the most dangerous part of backpacking. Never go into rushing water that is over your thighs! As an experienced river rat, I can assure you that the force is far greater than you can imagine.

Scout upstream and down for the safest crossing spot. Typically this is a wider spot in the creek where the current is slower. But be certain there are no immediate downstream hazards such as a water-fall or a strainer (fallen tree).

Do not attempt to cross barefoot; the cold water makes it easy to injure your feet without knowing it until too late. Either wear the sandals you brought for the occasion or wear your trail shoes or boots. Remove long pants to reduce water drag on your legs, unfasten the sternum strap on your pack, and keep the hip belt secure so you don't lose your balance.

It is generally best for one person to cross at a time while using a pair of trekking poles (a single pole is far inferior here). Cross sideways to the current, taking small steps, and move slightly downstream toward the opposite bank. Always keep three solid points of contact and use the poles to probe your way.

Other members of your group should be deployed downstream, ready to render assistance, but don't make the mistake of getting dragged in during a rescue attempt. If you have a rope, it should be used as a throw line; never tied around the waist. Hand lines can be misleadingly dangerous and are best avoided. Crossing as a group is a complex subject with more ways to do it wrong than right (hint: linking hands is always wrong!) so do not attempt without training.

If you do get swept off your feet, never try to stand up! This can result in a trapped foot and drowning. Instead, float on your back with your feet pointed downstream and work your way to shore.

Chapter Eight
Making Camp

Rolling into camp, your first thoughts are probably to relax before dealing with chores. Let me gently suggest that a better course of action is to drop your pack, perhaps toss on a warm layer, and deal with some of the necessities before you cool down. It's oh so much better to relax when you know you can really relax.

Sometimes you may wish to stop early, make dinner, and then hike a bit farther. This can save you hauling water, doesn't invite bears to visit your camp, and gives you more options on where to sleep.

ESTABLISHING CAMP

Typically, the first major chore is preparing your night haven. If possible, you want a site that isn't too far from the water that you will need for cooking but no closer than 200 feet. Sometimes a great view is wonderful, but those spots are often brutal in a storm. And camping near the trail is a bad idea because a tent is an eyesore for others and people will tramp past at ungodly hours.

When evaluating potential tent sites, look for a flat spot that will not become a lake if it rains; compacted soil in heavily used sites are prone to flooding. Digging a trench around your tent to divert runoff is absolutely forbidden because it is ineffective and those scars last for many years. Check overhead for "widow makers" (i.e., dead trees and branches that may fall in the wind) in forests. Though tempting, don't camp in creek beds, particularly in the desert, because a flash flood can ruin your night.

Once you've found the spot, clear out any rocks and branches that will poke holes in your tent. Pitch your tent, inflate your pad, and pull out your sleeping bag to loft up. This is a good time to change into warm, dry clothes for evening.

At this point, you may wish to fetch enough water for dinner and breakfast, decide where to locate your kitchen, and rig your food-hauling system. It is wise to put a good distance between your sleeping bag and all the things that smell tasty to critters. Cooking in one place, washing dishes in another, and hanging your food in yet another can decrease the likelihood of nighttime disturbances.

After dinner, you will need to hang your food and tidy up the campsite. Make sure that important things are protected against rain during the night. Have your headlamp and any other necessities (stocking hat, eyeglasses, etc.) laid out where you can reach them during the night. It helps to establish a routine so you can find things easily.

DINNER TIME

The lore of backpacking is filled with tales of dinners

ruined by pots tipping over due to unstable stoves. Do yourself a favor and take the time to locate a good spot for setting up your kitchen. Ideally you can find a large flat rock for your stove—bonus if it's on a ledge that you can hang your legs off while cooking—but you may need to clear a bit of ground of flammable leaves.

The two most important factors for speeding cooking and saving fuel are using a windscreen and keeping a lid on the pot. Other ways to conserve include heating items by placing them on the lid of the cooking pot and using a pot cozy (or wrapping with a towel) to keep a pot warm while the food hydrates.

Backpackers are frequently warned to never cook inside a tent. But the reality is that there are times when cooking outside is not an option. If possible, cook under the vestibule and far enough away from walls and sleeping bags to prevent melting. Always keep at least one large vent open and cook with extreme caution. If you are in grizzly country and anticipate rain, a separate cook fly is worth carrying.

When cooking, you may need to stir frequently to prevent burning because many stoves concentrate the heat (better pots help). Also tall, skinny pots need more stirring for even heating of the food.

After dinner, it is wise to clean dirty pots, bowls, and cups before things set up. Hot or warm water is best, but even cold water will suffice if used with biodegradable soap. Never wash dishes directly in a stream or pond! Always carry them 200 feet away and then broadcast the dishwater over a wide area. This applies to bathing too if you feel the need.

CRITTER COUNTRY

The more popular the backpacking destination, the bigger the problem with mice, ravens, raccoons, and bears. Many of the shelters on the East Coast are equipped with "mouse mobiles," which are strings with inverted empty cans to prevent rodents from reaching the goodies (like a squirrel guard on a bird

Bears are exciting to see in the backcountry, but you definitely don't want them getting into your food stash. Stephen Gorman

Where permitted, using a waterproof stuff sack and a throw bag (right) is a popular option for stowing food overnight. In areas where rodents and birds are the main threat to food, a steel mesh bag (front) is a reasonably light method for keeping critters at bay. Some parks require the use of bear canisters (left), but they are heavy and awkward to carry. A lighter alternative is to use a durable bag made of HMPE (rear) that bears cannot rip open. However, not all parks allow them.

feeder). Leave your pack unguarded with food inside and you may find a hole chewed in it.

You may think you are intelligent, but when it comes to reaching food bags, ravens, raccoons, and bears are smarter. Old tricks, like tossing a line over a limb and tying it to the trunk or stringing a line between two trees and hoisting food up the middle, are doomed to failure. Ravens know how to open zippers, and their beaks can go through thick plastic containers.

Although they are a nuisance to carry due to the awkward shape, bear cans combined with odor-tight storage bags are highly effective at deterring bruins. In several regions, you are required to use them. It's a good idea to add reflective tape so you can find the can after the bear has given up playing soccer. Where permitted, bear sacks are a lighter and easier-to-carry alternative that can be tied to a tree or rock.

If you want to hang food, you will need about 50 feet of cord attached to a tiny stuff sack, plus a mini-carabiner and a stick. Put a rock in the stuff sack and toss it over a limb that is at least 15 feet off the ground and 7 feet from tree trunks or large branches. Tie a loop in the line, clip the carabiner and food bag

Proper technique for hanging food.

to it, and then clip the free line. Now pull on the free line until the food bag is at the limb. Reach as high as you can and girth hitch the stick, then lower the food bag until the stick jams in the carabiner. This leaves your food hanging about 10 feet in the air, and it can be retrieved only by pulling down the cord.

BREAKING CAMP

Come dawn, start motivating and resist the urge to sleep in. Get dressed right away for the day's hike, with your sweater or jacket over top to fight off the chill. Coffee drinkers will want to get their brew going as soon as possible, and the rest of the group would be wise to humor their addiction. Retrieve your food bag and start heating a pot of water on the stove.

While water is heating for drinks and hot cereal, stuff your sleeping bag, roll up the sleeping pad, and stow away things you won't need during the day. By this time the water is probably boiling, so go enjoy breakfast.

Once breakfast is finished, clean up and pack away the kitchen and food. Take down your tent and return the area to a natural state. Also police the entire campsite for micro-trash.

Before you hit the trail, it will be time for your morning toilet break; that 2 pounds of food you consumed the day before is now 1 pound of feces. Some heavily used parks are requiring backpackers to carry out everything—yes, everything—and will provide bags for that purpose. Everywhere else you will need to dig a cathole about 6 to 8 inches deep and 6 inches in diameter. You can use a stick or tent stake but it does help to carry a small trowel for this purpose.

The site should be at least 200 feet from water and out of sight of trails; a bit of privacy is nice when taking a bio break. Do yourself a favor and make sure there is no poison ivy, poison oak, stinging nettles, or cactus in the vicinity! Be sure to bury everything and restore the site to natural.

As a more durable yet comfortable alternative to toilet paper, you might try thick half-size paper towels. Burning and burying toilet paper or paper towels is no longer recommended because neither method works well and "trekker prayer flags" often result as animals scatter unsanitary paper that takes years to break down. Carry two freezer bags to collect used toilet paper and tampons, then dispose of them when you reach the trailhead.

Chapter Nine
High, Cold Mountains

Backpacking above 10,000 feet presents a few challenges that can take a little getting used to . . . not the least of which is the thin air! You can also anticipate colder nights, snow at any time of year, and some issues when cooking.

Sadly for those coming from sea level, there are no shortcuts to acclimatizing. The best you can hope for is to alleviate some of the symptoms of altitude maladies with aspirin or ibuprofen. Those who suffer greatly may wish to use acetazolamide (Diamox), which is a prescription medication that helps relieve symptoms. While it isn't cheating, taking Diamox does not speed the body's adjustment to altitude. See my book *Climbing: Training for Peak Performance* for greater detail on preparation.

When you reach altitude, slow your normal pace down or you will soon find yourself gasping for breath. Going too high, too fast is what makes backpackers feel like they got run over by a train. Take your time, drink *lots* of fluids, and eat plenty of carbohydrates. Even if you've had mountain sickness in the past, it doesn't mean you will always get it. Unfortunately, the reverse is also true.

Because there is less atmosphere, the sun is much more intense, so you must be extra careful to

Slow down your normal pace when hiking at high elevation.
Stephen Gorman

wear sun protection. The glare off snow also requires greater eye protection than offered by standard sunglasses.

When hiking in the spring and early summer, you are likely to encounter deep snow in many places. Though you probably do not need insulated boots, you will likely need knee-high gaiters since you will be

Trekking poles are useful when crossing soft snowfields in the midday sun like this, but an ice ax and even crampons may be desired on hard, icy slopes. Stephen Gorman

post-holing. If it's a big snow year, you may even want to bring a small pair of snowshoes.

Early in the season, snowfields that need to be crossed often cover trails. You might be able to get away with just using your hiking poles for short sections, but a slip can send you rapidly sliding into rocks. This is a time when it can be well worth carrying a pair of lightweight crampons, such as Kahtoolas, for security on icy slopes. You may even want hiking poles with a self-arrest grip or an ice axe, which can also be used for chopping steps.

Although butane stoves perform better at higher altitude, this can be offset by decreased performance in the cold. Modern butane stoves with a preheat coil or pressure regulator are the most convenient. But if you are relying on melting snow as water for a group, you may wish to carry a reliable blowtorch-style white gas stove.

Regardless of the stove model, don't count on a piezo igniter or refillable lighter to work at high altitude. Simply carry a BIC disposable lighter and keep it warm in your pocket. When cooking on snow, you will either need a meltproof stove platform or a hanging kit for your stove.

Anticipate that it will take longer for water to boil. And due to the lower boiling temperature of water (193°F at 10,000 feet instead of 212°F at sea level), it will take longer for foods to cook or rehydrate. Fast-cooking starches (such as ramen, orzo, couscous, and instant rice) are a better option than spaghetti or normal rice.

Since nausea is fairly common for people with mountain sickness, carry some bland foods like oatmeal, soups, and crackers. Once your body adjusts, you can handle spicy foods again and may even crave fatty foods. Bring plenty of tea, instant cider, and hot chocolate to encourage hydrating at breakfast and dinner.

To prevent water from freezing at night, it is standard practice to bring a water bottle inside the sleeping bag; be certain that it will not leak. And to avoid crawling out of the tent at night, many campers carry a pee bottle; be certain it can't be mistaken for a water bottle during the night.

Chapter Ten

Hot Deserts

In contrast to the mountains, backpacking in the desert presents a different set of challenges . . . not the least of which is the heat! Of course, water is scarce and the nights can be surprisingly chilly. But desert hiking has its own rewards and should not be missed.

The best time to visit most deserts is in the spring and the fall; summers are just too brutally hot, and winters can be bitter. Far too many hikers underestimate how dangerous it is to work hard in hot weather. When the air temperature is above 95ºF, radiation, one of your primary mechanisms for reducing core temperature, is lost. This only leaves you with evaporation, and that too will soon be lost if you don't carry a lot of water.

For most times of the year when backpacking, you need a minimum of 5 liters of water per person per day; that is 11 pounds in your pack. Unless you plan your trips around *guaranteed* water supplies or bury caches ahead of time, you will be limited to how long you can stay out.

In very hot weather, choose loose-fitting, light-colored clothing that has long sleeves. Many desert hikers prefer cotton because it absorbs water and evaporates more slowly than synthetics. Definitely

Don't be afraid of snakes when hiking in the desert, but do watch where you step. Stephen Gorman

wear a hat with a full, wide brim, not just a baseball cap.

Avoid hiking in the hottest part of the day (mid-afternoon), go at a slow pace and rest frequently, and take sips of water every fifteen minutes. During the day, be sure to drink fluids with electrolytes to replace what is lost in sweat. Due to the risk of heat exhaustion and heat stroke, which can sneak up with little warning, always hike with a partner so you can monitor each other's condition.

Contrary to popular belief, you pretty much have to work at getting bitten by a rattlesnake. Aside from the generous warning they provide, they don't tend to be aggressive unless provoked. Watch where you step, don't make them mad, and you'll be fine. Ignore those rules and you're on the way to the ER, in a slow, controlled manner; getting bit may hurt like heck, but adults won't die if they receive proper treatment. Don't bother carrying snakebite kits and ignore cut-and-suck folklore since none of that works and actually causes more problems.

Be careful to avoid brushing against cactus or you may spend an hour plucking out needles. It is wise to carry a multi-tool with needle-nosed pliers, as well as splinter tweezers, for this unpleasant task.

When making camp, do not pitch your tent in an arroyo (dry creek bed) if there is even a hint of rain in the distance. All too often, a storm that is miles away can send a flash flood roaring down. Backpacking through slot canyons can be very dangerous in the spring when storms are most common.

After you select a campsite, get everything ready but leave your sleeping bag stuffed to prevent sharing your bag with a scorpion. Some backpackers carry an ultraviolet flashlight to spot scorpions at night.

Chapter Eleven
Backcountry Adversity

The best equipment in the world cannot ensure a positive experience on a backpacking trip. Nor can wisdom earned or wisdom learned. Ultimately, what really determines whether you have a great trip, no matter the amount of adversity, is your attitude.

A good friend of mine, Erik Weihenmayer, speaks of using "positive pessimism" in the face of adversity as a tool to not only overcome problems but also shatter perceived barriers. By this he means that you acknowledge the severity of the situation, preferably with a joke, and immediately move on to achieving a desirable outcome. Erik knows a little more about overcoming adversity than most of us—he is the only blind person to climb the Seven Summits, the highest peak on each continent (www.touchthetop.com).

The reality is that you *will* run into problems out on the trail. You can, and should, prepare for good times and bad (see the *Backpacker Magazine* companion book *Trailside First Aid*). But the very nature of backpacking dictates that there will be discomfort and inconvenience along the way—if you can't handle that concept, stick to four-star hotels. Sometimes things can be severe, and that's when your attitude toward adversity makes a huge difference.

Whine and be miserable or think positive and make things better.

Remember too that attitudes are contagious. If you emanate a bad vibe, that can spread to others in your group, compounding everyone's misery. On the other hand, you also have the power to boost the group's psychology and overcome adversities with a bright attitude.

Backpacking is an absolutely great recreation. Carrying your home on your back for a few days, or a few weeks, can take you away from the "real world" and get you into mind-blowing locations. Backpacking is an activity suitable for able and disabled bodies, young and old. Hikes can be equally enjoyable with family, friends, or alone. It can be a "gateway drug" to climbing and kayaking, mountaineering and rafting, biking and skiing, as well as adventure travel.

As with all activities, there is a learning curve to living on the trail. Hopefully this book will shorten that part of the experience so you can enjoy the rest of it for decades to come.

Index